THIS MAGIC SCARF BOOK

BELONGS TO

YUMMY COCONUT CAKE

IN THE OVEN HOW LONG WILL IT TAKE?

HURRY AND BAKE, I CAN''T WAIT

MY FAVOURITE COCONUT CAKE

My Magic Scarf

Copyright © 2015 by Robyn Smart

Cover Design © by R Scott. All Rights Reserved.

First Edition 2015

First Printing 2015

All rights reserved. No part of this publication may be reproduced, distributed, or transmitted in any form or by any means, including photocopying, recording, or other electronic or mechanical methods, without the prior written permission of the publisher and copyright owner, except in the case of brief quotations embodied in critical reviews and certain other non-commercial uses permitted by copyright law.

This novel is a work of fiction.

Names, characters, places and incidents are a product of the author's imagination or used fictionally. Any resemblance to actual events, locales, or persons, living or dead, is purely coincidental.

Tanya rushed from the garden into her bedroom. She wanted to change her shoes before her mum could see the scuffs she had made on them, by kicking large stones in a game she often played with her brother.

As Tanya sat on the floor to tie her laces, she felt a sharp pain in her belly. Always this silly pain thought Tanya.
She never mentioned it to her parents.

Running down the stairs Tanya could smell her favourite cake.
Mmm yummy coconut cake.

As she got nearer to the kitchen, Tanya could see the hem of her mum's colourful skirt swishing from corner to corner.

Her mother always wore brightly coloured skirts, she said they lifted her mood.

Tanya entered the kitchen singing: -

YUMMY
COCONUT
CAKE
IN THE OVEN
HOW LONG
WILL IT
TAKE?
HURRY AND
BAKE, I
CAN"T WAIT

MY
FAVOURITE
COCONUT
CAKE

Tanya could see the elaborate design on her mother's skirt.
Its colours dazzled as the sun shone through the window.
She also had the scarf to match.

The scarf was tied neatly, with folds and curves tucked to form a neat wrap on her head. As her mother turned around she had a bright smile on her face.

After what seemed like a lifetime the cake was baked.
Tanya and her brother Tarique both raced into the kitchen.

On the kitchen counter lay the coconut cake, still steaming.

Mum had decorated the top with chocolate sprinkles.

Hmm Yummy. As Tanya ate the cake she started to feel sick.

She swallowed the first bite and began to convince

herself that she could even go for another slice.

With each bite, Tanya began to feel even more sick.
This was not good she thought. She was SOOO looking forward

to eating her favourite coconut cake.

Looking around to see where her mother was Tanya called out

"MUUUUUM, I feel ……………."

The words did not come out properly and Tanya threw up everywhere. It was not a nice sight.

Tanya's legs felt weak. Her whole body felt weak.

Her mother clasped her arms around her body and led Tanya upstairs to bed.

Tanya fell asleep almost straight away and only woke up when she heard a noise in her room.

Tanya woke up to the chirping of the birds the following morning.

Surely she would be feeling better now, but in fact she was feeling worse.

She looked around and there sitting on the floor next to her bed was her brother Tarique.

His headphones glued to his ears as usual. Oh well at least she had company.

Shortly afterwards her door opened slowly with her mum appearing, carrying her favourite teddy bear Buggles in one hand and a cup in the other.

Placing the teddy bear next to Tanya and the cup on the table, she leaned over to give her a gentle hug.

"Tanya," her mum said soothingly, "You will be fine."
At that point her mother began to sing.

Mummy girl not feeling well,
Eat too much cake and her belly swell.
Don't you worry little girl of mine,
In a few days you'll be feeling fine.

You will be fine

But as the days went past, Tanya became worse.

Tanya's mother and father came into her room.

She bent over Tanya, pulling both her eyes down and asking her to stick out her tongue.

Shaking, her mother felt Tanya's head. After sticking her tongue out Tanya managed to find her voice although her throat was very dry.

"I still don't feel well and I can't move my legs and my tummy still hurts."

Tanya's dad stood up straight.

"Corrine ring de Doctor!"

Tanya's mother responded in a high pitched voice, one she saved for surprises or times of shock.

"De doctor, does she really need a doctor?"

"Yes Corrine" replied her father,
"De girl said she can't move her legs and she feels sick and that dark brown skin of hers looking peaky, just call de doctor."

"Yes Doctor, she does feel a little bit hot and she looks a bit off colour, well you know what I mean, and she says she can't move her legs so we are very worried."

"An ambulance! Ok well thank you Doctor." Tanya's dad looked at her mother nervously.

"Well what did he say?"

"He said he's sending an ambulance right now."

"Let's get her ready," said Tanya's dad.

He began to move quickly, gathering her gown, slippers and a small toiletry bag for her toothbrush, face flannel and a towel.

In the meantime, Tanya's mum picked up the phone to ring Grandma Brown to ask if she could collect Tarique from school.

Tanya could hear her Grandmother on the other end of the phone.

**"WHAT YOU SEY, SHE CAN'T MOVE HER LEGS,
HOW YOU MEAN SHE CAN'T MOVE HER LEGS?"**

Tanya's grandmother had a habit of repeating her words.
Maybe she thought people didn't hear the first time around.

"SO YOU SEY, SHE CAN'T MOVE HER LEGS? YES MAN TEK HER TO THE HOSPITAL, QUICK!"

As Tanya's grandmother continued to repeat herself, her dad seemed to be getting impatient.

"Corinne please we don't have time to chat, mek we hurry and get the chile ready."

"Mamma Brown I have to go now, the ambulance will be here shortly, we will talk later, don't forget to pick up Tarique please."

Before they knew it the ambulance arrived.

Tanya could hear voices downstairs; her dad was explaining to the ambulance men what had happened.

The ambulance men came up to her room ready to take her to the hospital.

As she was placed onto the hard stretcher in the ambulance, she could hear raised voices outside.

It was her parents. Her dad's voice sounded stern and Tanya became nervous.

"Corinne you go in the ambulance and I will follow behind in de car, you can't drive can you?
No! so gwarn in the ambulance quick, you wasting time."

Tanya's mum climbed into the ambulance and took her place on a very small seat holding Tanya's hand so tightly that she nearly cut off her circulation.

Within minutes they had arrived at the hospital.

The rear door was opened and Tanya was wheeled into the hospital where she was met by a nurse. The hospital was busy and loud.

Tanya was cold and pulled her dressing gown around her.

As she did so, the nurse asked her to roll her sleeve up. She went away and came back with a funny looking machine and placed it around Tanya's arm and turned it on with a touch of a button.

The nurse said the machine was taking Tanya's blood pressure then said she was going to take some blood.

Tanya looked at her mother who looked as though she was about to faint.

"Just a gentle prick," the nurse said reassuringly. Tanya began to sweat, more so with panic.

At that point her dad's face appeared around the curtain.

The nurse explained that the doctors would be with them shortly. Both her parents sat down on hard grey chairs.

A few minutes later the doctors appeared.

The one in the front seemed to be in charge.

His glasses perched on the edge of his nose.

"Mr Brown could we have a word with you outside please."

Tanya's dad got up slowly. She could hear him cough slightly but she could not hear much more until
he returned and beckoned for her mother to go outside and he came in.

When Tanya's dad sat down, he didn't even look at Tanya but lowered his head into his hands.

When he raised his head it appeared he had been crying. His eyes were red and he was sniffling.
The doctor said they would need to put a drip in with medicine to help the pain.
In the meantime, they took Tanya's temperature.

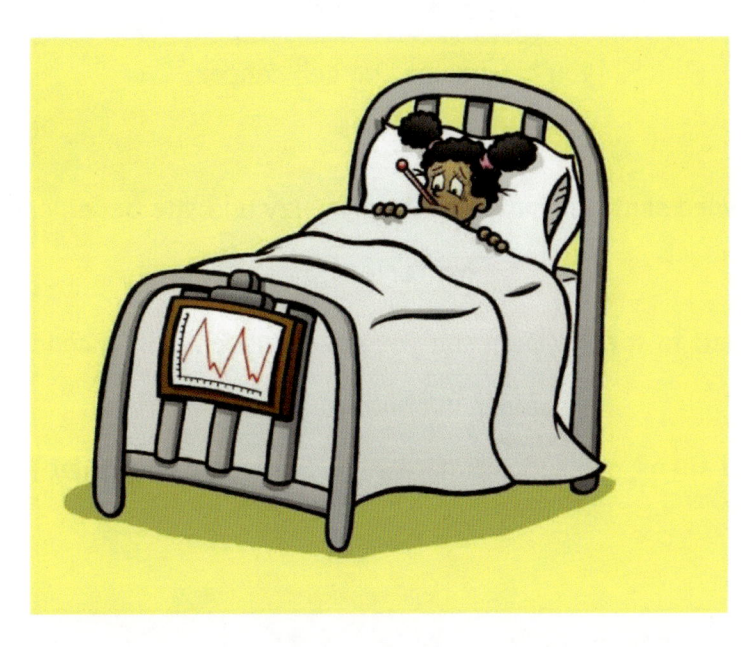

Tanya asked her dad what a drip was.

"It's a bottle of medicine baby, to help de pain but it goes straight inna de body quick."

Tanya's mum returned fixing her scarf and wiping her eyes and looking nervous.

"Corrine sit now no man!" said Tanya's dad," we need to explain to Tanya what de doctor sey."
"Oh yes" replied her mother.
Tanya's dad then cleared his throat as if to speak, then paused.

"Tanya, you sick, I mean you sick bad but de doctors can fix it, dem seh you have someting call cancer."

The very word sent her mother into a frenzy and she began crying hysterically.
He continued to speak. "Dem seh you have leukaemia, it a cancer what is popular in children of your age."
Tanya stayed silent, not sure what to say. "So dad how do they fix it?"

"With medicine like when I have a cold?" asked Tanya, "Some ting like dat Tanya, some ting like dat."

Tanya was admitted to the hospital and it was a while before she saw her mother again.

Her father seemed to take charge like he always did in emergency situations.

The following days were filled with seeing more doctors called Oncologists. They are doctors who deal with cancer.

Oncologists was a big word for Tanya to pronounce, so she just called them **Oncolo's**.

The days in hospital became boring. Tanya spent most of her days colouring.

Tanya wanted to see Tarique, in fact she almost missed him.

Tanya's dad explained that Tarique could not come to see her.

"Well Tarique has a cold Tanya and because of your illness he can't come up because dem seh your immune system low."

A few days later Tanya was told that she was about to be started on chemotherapy.

The Oncolo's explained that this was a medicine that would zap the cancer and hopefully make Tanya better.

The zapping day as they called it was planned for the following day.

Tanya was given anti sickness medicine beforehand to stop her from being sick.

Grandma Brown came up a few hours before the zapping took place and in usual grandma fashion kept repeating herself.

"I CAN'T BELIEVE THIS LITTLE GIRL HAVE CANCER, I MEAN ONLY BIG PEOPLE GET CANCER NOT LITTLE PEOPLE, I MEAN I JUST CAN'T BELIEVE IT."

Tanya's dad tried to get Grandma Brown to talk quietly but she began to talk even louder. "CANCER, NO MAN !"

Grandma was led gently off the ward blowing Tanya a kiss which made her false teeth fall out.

For the first time in days Tanya chuckled.

The zapping day arrived and Tanya had a knot in her stomach, she felt sick with fear.

The doctors came around to explain would happen next.

They told her she would feel tired when she had the medication but worst of all that she was going to lose her hair.

Dad suggested that they all shave their hair to support Tanya.
He brought his shaver to the hospital.

Gently holding Tanya's head, he began to shave her beautiful long hair, then his, then her mothers.

Tanya looked in the mirror and began to cry. Her long ponytails had gone.

Seeing Tanya crying really upset her parents.

Her mum then said, "Tanya behind every dark cloud is a silver lining, and your silver lining is that you can wear the same scarfs as me."

"I mean you always sey I look nice and bright, well you can look nice and bright as well,

we will look almost like twins. I can just see it now."

"A magic scarf that will brighten your day and make the miserable days go away.

Your friends will be jealous."

Tanya imagined herself wearing bright and scarfs.

"Could I wear them to school?" she asked her mum.

"Of course you can" she replied.

Within the next few weeks following her treatment, Tanya went back to school. She dreaded it, but her mum went to a meeting with the head teacher.

Her mum explained that Tanya couldn't take part in sports for the moment but she could keep scores.

Tanya also had to be careful around other children who had colds, her immune system was still low.

If children did have any colds, they would have to tell the teacher.

On the Friday of her first week back to school, Tanya's teacher decided to hold a special assembly for her.

She explained to the children why Tanya had been in hospital and why she wore a scarf and how the children could help her in school.

At first Tanya felt shy but then as she stood up she felt: -

MAGICAL

The scarf had a beautiful pattern with different shades and colours.
Tanya looked in the window and smiled at her reflection.
She didn't EVER want to take this one off.

But then again her mother had made her lots more. So each day she could pick another one.

As Tanya timidly walked to the front of the assembly she heard a door open.

There stood a group of children and teachers also wearing hats and scarfs walking into the hall.

Tanya no longer felt like the odd one out, she felt special in her

MAGICAL SCARF

Printed in Great Britain
by Amazon